HOPE = BOLD

10 Day Study for a New Reality

By Eric Reeder

ISBN-13:978-1974607471

ISBN-10:197460747X

Scripture references from ESV unless otherwise noted.
The Holy Bible, English Standard Version® (ESV®)
Copyright © 2001 by Crossway,
a publishing ministry of Good News Publishers.
All rights reserved.
ESV Text Edition: 2016

www.wearethehopeful.com

About the Author::

Eric Reeder -
Founder of We Are The Hopeful
President of RISEmovement Inc.
Itinerate and conference speaker
Author and blogger
For details of the various emphases Eric leads, see
www.wearethehopeful.com

Eric has influenced and shaped mindsets of people all over the world. From those battling addiction to CEO's, from young adults to seniors, from occasional church-attenders to those leading congregations, he has helped many understand key realities that put life on a trajectory to thrive. With more than 2 decades of leadership in various fields he has a unique ability to impact people right where they are. His in-depth study and creative processing gives him perspectives that challenge the status quo.

He is driven to articulate **The HOPE-filled Gospel** to unveil God as a good Father & unlock who we really are. He is passionate about his dream for a Hope Revolution.

The greatest injustice is a heart left fatherless. It

i

is the epidemic of history and the premiere source of brokenness in our society. Removing the fear-based concept of God as angry and harsh, and awakening hearts to the good Father Jesus revealed, is the solution that relieves hearts, renovates culture, and raises the bar so we develop a brighter future.

With 20+ years of marriage, Eric and Angela are consumed with unveiling the goodness of Father and releasing The HOPE-filled Gospel around the world. They are raising 4 children, and also walking with spiritual sons and daughters who are leading the charge of THE HOPE REVOLUTION. Their real-life, authentic heart for meaningful relationships inspire many to be their true selves.

They live in the small town of Belpre, OH with their children, Ezekiel, Nehemiah, Lizzie, and Liberty.

Dedication ::

To the one who is dying for a new reality, to
the one looking to rise into beauty despite all
the ashes:

This is for you. This is for hearts ready to
embrace something for NOW instead of
putting it off until later. This book is for the
one ready for a download that upgrades your
understanding of what's available to you.

Contents ::

Introduction ::

Hope unlocks boldness which releases courage to do what you thought you never could...

Hope is a force required to make the needed changes that lead to improvement and achievement. To go forward demands new mindsets that bring forth different actions, fresh ideas, more creativity, and fuller function. Coming to understand hope, what it is, where it comes from, and how it changes things is your key to living bold.

Over the next 10 days you have the opportunity to receive a new download on hope, an upgrade. You will find some life-changing "ah-ha" moments that fuel your day-to-day life. This 10 Day Study isn't the full scope on hope. My aim is to provide you some shortened insights that can bring you a fresh encounter in hope. You will want to continue to gain more through my other resources. It will enable you to advance into a new reality.

Here are some statements on hope to get your mind thinking and open your heart:

- Hope must be solidified and never again be understood from the unsecured frailties of a wish.
- Hope eclipses a wish.
- Hope moves us. A wish stagnates us. Leaves us guessing.
- Hope takes away the questioning.
- Hope is set from what already IS, while a wish is based on what want to come.

For most, hope has been understood as a desire for something you want. That understanding is more like a wish. I want to take you beyond that concept because a wish or a want is unstable and isn't a foundation upon which we build.

We are to build on a rock not sand.

My desire is that you have a solid place in your heart and mind that can sustain you and fuel you no matter what comes toward you in life. Starting from these points will be of great strength to you:

- Hope is solid.
- Hope is secure.
- Hope is unwavering.
- Hope inspires full dedication.

- Hope sustains.
- Hope produces boldness.

Too often, hope gets communicated like an inspirational greeting card. Because of that, hope gets placed into the category of positive thinking. Positive thinking is good, right, and needed, but these statements will help us see hope is the source of positive thinking and optimism:

- Hope isn't positive thinking but causes it.
- Hope isn't optimistic feelings, but creates them.

Because so many hearts and minds struggle with thinking positive or being optimistic, hope can be toss out by "logic" and often said to be for those that want to ignore things or hide from "reality". When hope is more correctly understood, that line of thinking becomes obsolete. Then hope becomes understood as reality. Coming to that conclusion then reveals that to deny hope is actually hiding from reality. Here are a few ways we can say that:

- Hope isn't closing your eyes to situations. It's a different way of understanding them.

- Hope is a means of interruption, a grid through which you look.
- Hope empowers you to go forward. A wish tricks you into staying.
- Hope stands when everything else falls.
- Hope was here before things started, and hope will be at the end.

Our challenge is to move away from hope being connected to a wish. Our culture mostly uses the word hope when it'd be more accurate to say "wish or want". Because that has been done for so long, our minds have been trained to see hope more about something we don't have yet. This is unfortunate because it removes us from experiencing the force that hope really is.

In this book, I am going to reveal hope is way beyond a wish. I want to help you have a new understanding that hope is not about a "maybe" or "it might". Hope is about an assurance and something secure.

You will see hope is not based on what you want or would like. Hope is what is available through love. When you come to understand what hope really is it will unlock in you the boldness you need to be the truest you.

> **Hope isn't closing your eyes to situations. It's a different way of under-standing.**

I'm excited for you to experience what this book offers you. Many are being awakened to the present reality of hope and moving away from understanding hope has to do with the future only.

I have made this a 10 day study because the number 10 has unique symbolism for "divine order". It gives a picture of completeness or something finished. It is the end of one set of numbers that gives way to the start of another. This is because you are coming to the end of one way of thinking and coming into a new mindset for a new reality.

Over the next 10 days you will end some ways you've understood hope and gain what's needed for you to go forward in a new reality.

There will be old ways of thinking that will crumble and end giving way to new understanding. And this will be a new way of thinking for you to adapt to for a more suitable way of living.

When you get through these 10 days, I want you to start over and read again. Then, read again so you end up with a month's worth of renewing your heart and mind. Repetition is needed for living bold. I have provided you space within the book to make notes from what you are realizing and coming to understand. I have also left space for your "Before and After". I ask you a question at the end of each day to make note of where you are before you've finished the book. Then, later you look back and see what you've gained after reading. So keep this before you and also look for other materials I have provided at www.wearethehopeful.com.

Living in a new reality through hope produces a bold life!

Your Notes ::

Before and After ::

Take a few minutes to write where you are right now with hope.
You'll be able to look back later and see how you've grown.
Write down areas you right now that need you to embrace hope.

"Since we have such a hope, we are very bold,"

2 Corinthians 3:12

HOPE = BOLD

Day 1 – *The Frailties of a Wish*

We get to live from something much more solid than a wish. A wish never drives anyone to do anything. A wish is about things that are not yet. Hope is based on what already is.

Most of the time, people say the word hope when what they mean is wish or want. Hope is not a want. Hope is not a wish. Because we continually hear the word hope in the context of a wish, the force and power of what hope is gets reduced. People say, "I hope you have a good day". They say, "I hope it doesn't rain today" or "I hope I get this for Christmas". These statements are not what hope is. These statements lower the reality of hope to the understanding of a wish. Don't live in the frailties of a wish.

> **A wish is about things that are not yet. Hope is about what already is.**

No one gives everything they are for a wish. A wish doesn't have innate power. Hope does! Hope is a force. Living life from a wish often leaves you disappointed. The wish you have lacks the force to move you into what you are wishing for. For example, I wish I could play the piano, but I have never done anything about that. A wish doesn't move us into action.

A wish leaves us deserted in an insecure place because we aren't sure if it'll happen. Hope is secure because hope is based on what has already happened. Hope isn't about what WILL happen. Hope is about what HAS happened, and what has happened is God's goodness prevailed. Understanding that reality of hope unlocks boldness. A wish leaves you wondering. Hope leaves you assured. Those are very different places from which to live.

You don't have to build life on the soft sands of a wish. You can build your heart and mind on the solid place of hope. This will be reflected in the way you *experience* life and the way you *contribute* to life. It will adjust your motives and answer fears. Hope is a reality we have. Hope is not something we are waiting on. That is your key in seeing hope differently.

Hope eclipses a wish.

Hope moves us. A wish stagnates us.

A wish leaves us guessing. Hope takes away the

question.

Hope is the unconditional assurance Father's goodness prevails. That is not a concept we are waiting on. It's a reality that we have. That is why I say hope is based on what has already happened instead of something waiting to happen. His goodness has already happened, and His goodness is already toward us. This is the secure place from which we live. When we embrace God is a good Father our hearts and minds are shaped by hope and we respond by living accordingly. We get to approach life FROM hope; from the unconditional assurance Father's goodness prevails.

> ...hope unlocks boldness. A wish leaves you wondering. Hope leaves you assured.

2 Corinthians 3:12 tells us "we HAVE this hope, so we are bold". Boldness is the result of hope. Instability is the result of a wish. The goodness of God is the assurance we have. The assurance that His goodness prevails is the anchor of our souls. This is hope.

Today, hope is yours. You have what is needed

because you have hope. Hope is here.

Be Bold.

Your Notes ::

Before and After ::

Where have you been wishing rather than being in hope?

"**And we all, with unveiled faces, beholding the glory of the Lord, are being transformed...**"

2 Corinthians 3:18

Day 2 - *Behold = Become*

The images we put before us shape us in many ways. What we look at, consider, contemplate, study, and behold, we become. What we see, we hold as true. Our seeing, often times, needs to go beyond the physical because the non-physical is the origin. We have capacity to see in multiple realms. We see in many ways. We perceive, we estimate, and we presume. Each of those are a type of sight. A kind of beholding. What you are beholding is what you are becoming. Your ability to perceive is based from what you behold. Sometimes we perceive well and other times not so well. That's why it is vital to investigate what you are beholding.

> **When we behold Jesus we get to see the full, true image of God.**

In Mark 8, Jesus healed a blind man and his first sight was seeing men as trees. Jesus touched him again and he saw clearly. This can tell us there are times we need multiple efforts to see correctly. In order to see clearly, we need to keep going back to Jesus so we can see more and more of His nature. From that, we can understand ourselves more fully.

2 Corinthians 3:18 says we are those who "behold Him with unveiled faces". We get to see God without distortion. We get to be without barriers. Moses was afraid that if he saw God he would die. Then Apostle Paul tells us we see Him unrestricted. We get to see Him without dying. When we behold Him, its freedom. We are freed from wrong thinking of Him. We are freed from wrong thinking of ourselves. We are freed from wrong concepts, presumptions, and assumptions that He's somehow angry or harsh. When we behold Jesus we get to see the full, true image of God.

In continual beholding we gain constant becoming. However you see God is what you become. If you see Him angry, you'll more easily be angry. If you see Him happy, you'll more easily be happy. If you see Him withholding from you, you'll more easily withhold from yourself and others. If you see Him freely giving without strings, you'll give freely without strings.

This requires that we see hope differently. This may mean we need additional touches from Jesus to bring true hope into focus. To see hope is to see His goodness. His goodness is a solid, constant reality. Hope is not optimism or positive thinking. Hope is to

> **In continual beholding we gain constant becoming.**

behold the goodness that is the outworking of love. He is actually so good that He allows us to behold Him, so we know how good He is. When we behold Him as a good Father as Jesus showed, hope becomes our reality. His goodness is to be our beholding and our measure of beauty.

You will be what you see of Him, so see clearly; look at Jesus.

Behold boldly.

Your Notes ::

Before and After ::

Where have you been wishing rather than being in hope?

"Do not be anxious about anything..."

Philippians 4:6

Day 3 - *Today's Option*

Hope requires trust. Trust is a significant issue for many. Lack of trust makes hope a real challenge. Day after day we wake up with options. We either go at the day recoiled and holding our heart closed off, bracing for the worst, or we extend our heart to be vulnerable; so we enjoy freedom. Because hope is an unconditional assurance Father's goodness prevails, we have to investigate where we put our trust. Father's goodness is the product of love, but if we don't embrace the fact that goodness is His heart toward us, we miss that reality. The result is we live from the position of fear.

> **Hope is based on the goodness of God's love.**

Fear is limiting. Hope is boundless. Both fear and hope require trust. Fear demands trust. It's called anxiety. That's where trust is placed in a negative outcome or the possibility of a negative outcome. When we live in anxiety, we live bracing ourselves for the bottom to fall out from under us. We are trusting a crash is coming. This causes us to live restrained

> **Things we have anxiety over may or may not happen. But Father's goodness is for sure.**

because we never want to give our all just to have it all fall apart. We then end up just doing enough to get by feeling that's better because we won't "lose" as much when the crash happens. We were not designed or intended to live in anxiety; trusting in the negative. The tension, worry and stress this produces is like dissonance in our soul. It ongoingly causes our mind and body to function at lower levels. We don't have to live that way.

When we see hope differently than a wish or optimism, we can realize we have a solid place to put our trust. A wish and optimism are unstable. It's like living in a continual "maybe". Positive thinking rests on how well we can discipline our thinking and feelings. Hope isn't based on us or our ability to change our thinking. Hope is based on the goodness of God's love. Awakening to that changes our thinking. Then, we are different and we realize we can really park our trust on the unprecedented and unshakable love of our good Father. This becomes a liberating proposition to step further, every day, into deeper trust in the assurance His goodness prevails. This is the hope we have, so we are bold (2 Corinthians 3:12). Hope is what we get to live from. We live trusting His goodness is toward us and that goodness prevails.

Things we have anxiety over may or may not happen. But Father's goodness is for sure. Put your trust where it's solid. Watch boldness go to stronger measures in the way you love, how you dream, your mode of living and the intensity of your pursuits.

Today, you have options.

Live boldly.

Your Notes ::

Before and After ::

Is anxiety easier to embrace than hope, why or why not?

"Three things will last forever—faith, hope, and love...,"

1 Corinthians 13:13 (NLT)

Day 4 - *Hope Isn't Brief*

We all have ups and downs. We have days when our emotions, focus, and drive are stronger than others. We get tired. We get empty. Living in Spirit, with Father, through Jesus, is never a condemning situation, and you are not something less on the days that feel like a struggle. Those weak days are actually the days the strength of His goodness are most realized. We can't self-condemn when we are not achieving all we desire. Those are the times we rest in His goodness because we have an unconditional assurance in it.

> **Hope isn't a flash is the pan.**

With that said, it's important to see hope differently, in that it's not brief. It's not up one day and down the next. Hope can't go up or go down. It's constant and consistent. Our embrace of it, or our grip on it, may go up or down. Some may turn their backs on hope or may have never seen it, but hope isn't momentary. Hope is a glorious aspect of the Eternal who continually draws us into further glory.

2 Corinthians 3:7 gives us the account of how Moses' face shown with bright glory upon having the Law, but it was brief. I've found it to be true, that whenever

we start to improve ourselves with stronger efforts of our ability, it has a sense of glory. Like the feeling you're able to do it. It pushes a button in us that we like to know "we've got this". It makes us hold our head up higher. Ego, self-sufficiency, and pride enjoy this moment of "shining glory". But it's a brief glory. It starts at its best and declines from there. Living from self-reliance has a brief moment that feels like glory, but it never sustains. The Law Moses had is a picture of our efforts to obtain something from God. It speaks of the requirements we have to achieve. We jump into doing more, thinking it will make Him happy and things seem to be bright and at a high point. But we eventually discover we can't hold up or keep up. It becomes a point of condemnation for not being able to live up to this. We begin to fall back and usually our hearts lose a sense of glory. Things get cloudy and it seems harder to see how it can be better again. At that point it's like we need a "revival". We feel distance, less than before, and like we've done something wrong that's made Him mad so He backed up from us. This is the path of law and self-sufficient, performance living, but that kind of life doesn't have to be our life (2 Corinthians 3).

Unlike Moses, we have this hope and are able to behold Father with unveiled faces so Spirit leads us into further liberty. This moves us from living the "glory" of self-reliance to living His glory in the Spirit. The liberty Spirit gives us moves us from a fading glory to an everlasting glory (2 Corinthians 3:18). Life in Christ is not designed to be a cycle of life in glory and then to decline and then back to revival, back to decline with the conclusion of "never mind this doesn't work".

> **We are bold enough to enjoy the hope-filled relationship with Father.**

Like I said at the start, we all have tough days or tough seasons, but even in that we experience more glory as we live in this hope. We are bold enough to consider we can live lying in green pastures. We are bold enough to have dinner in the midst of battle (Psalms 23). We are not those living in the briefness of self-reliance and performance based interaction with God. We are bold enough to enjoy the hope-filled relationship with Father. We are the ones living the permanent, ever-advancing glory of a life without a veil. The Law showed us a brief glory that faded, but Jesus showed us the immeasurable, everlasting glory of Father's goodness.

Hope isn't brief. Hope is constant. Hope isn't a fading situation. Hope is eternal (1 Corinthians 13:13). Don't live in Moses. Live in Jesus.

Everlasting boldness!

Your Notes ::

Before and After ::

Do tough times cause you to feel your hope is down?

"Where the Spirit of the Lord is, there is freedom."

2 Corinthians 3:17

Day 5 - *Old Ways, Old Results*

400 years of slavery. 400 years of being under the whip of a tyrant, Pharaoh. Do what you're told or be punishment was the reality of 4 centuries. 400 years of never owning or having their own stuff. Generation after generation shaped in the mindset of full obedience or dire reaction. At times, the Israelites' supplies were reduced by Pharaoh but the demand of production increased, and if the quota wasn't met, a lashing.

This is the state in which Israel lived, under Egyptian rule. I'm not trying to provide exact number of years in slavery, but provide the context of long term mindsets. You can imagine the entrenched stronghold of slavery that controlled their thinking. They only understood that you "obey" and get a peaceful night or fail and get beaten. No mercy. No grace. Only rules and requirements to appease Pharaoh. Centuries of this forces a people to only see through a master/slave understanding. They only understood Conqueror and Conquered. The Conquered was required to obey in order to survive or have life, and in life it was only to serve and do what pleases the Conqueror otherwise, life ended.

> **He wants each one to hear His voice and know His heart.**

It is in this setting that God brought deliverance. He cleared the way. He ended the tyranny. He liberated and made an unprecedented offer. At the bottom of Mt Sinai, He invited all of Israel to the top (Exodus 19-20).

He wants each one to hear His voice and know His heart. He wanted them to know His goodness toward them and that He was placing them high above life as a slave. He broke Pharaoh's hold, He opened the water and He abolished the enemy army in the Red Sea. All this to show slaves that they are loved, wanted and able to live above.

Even with all the barriers and bondages removed, old mindsets kept them all at the bottom of the mountain. They were captured by fear and it held them from what was available. Old ways produced old results. They wanted to stay in a rule and law based system to find a sense of security. They wanted a list to live by so they could stay away from punishment they expected to receive due to failing keep the rules.

Hope was calling them to the top. Hope is always calling us up. We need to step beyond old ways of slave thinking. His goodness has prevailed. Pharaoh systems are broken. Barriers are opened. Enemies are at the bottom of the sea. Live from above, not under looking up.

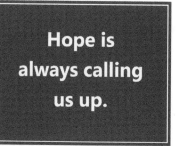

Hope is always calling us up.

Jesus was the revelation that punishment wasn't the nature of Father. The Law required punishment and the Law was the result of slave-thinking. Jesus shows us we are not slaves, we are sons and daughters with a Father full of grace, mercy and goodness toward us, that trumps punishment (James 2:13).

Hope calls us beyond old mindsets of slavery and awakens the realities of sonship. You've been freed. Don't live the Pharaoh performance-based way of life. You're called to live above that.

Embrace Father's invitation with boldness!

Your Notes ::

Before and After ::

What aspects of a "slave" mindset do you need to let go of?

HOPE = BOLD

"We have..."

2 Corinthians 3:12

HOPE = BOLD

Day 6 - *Receiving Not Chasing*

The reality that Father's goodness prevails is to say "hope is here". His goodness isn't coming, it's here. We are not chasing His goodness. We are in it. We are those in Christ and that assures us we have this hope (2 Corithians 3:12). What we must come to realize is that we are not OUT and NEEDING IN. Father's goodness is already toward us, and the situation is we are IN and we HAVE.

This is a significant change in thinking. It starts with considering: is hope is a future thing or a present thing? Hope is often incorrectly communicated as positive thinking and a wish. We mostly use the word hope for things we want. That frames our thinking to see hope as connected to things we don't have. Wanting is a response to not having.

> **When hope is put off till later it makes our hearts sick.**

When the word hope is used in conjunction with our desire of wanting it strips its present reality.

It's important to consider, do you live life receiving or chasing? A life of chasing is not a life parked on the present reality of Father's goodness prevailing. It's living a life wanting and feeling unsettled. It is a life of "not there yet". This puts our hearts in the place of striving in order to obtain. Fear and anxiety become our close friends when we live wanting. We constantly hear a voice telling us we'll never have and usually right behind that is a voice telling us we're not good enough to have it.

When we understand the present reality of hope and embrace Father's goodness is currently toward us, we get to have a heart enjoying a life of receiving. We become aware that Father has goodness coming toward us. We realize we are already IN not trying to get in. This reshapes the condition of our heart and changes our thinking. Proverbs 13:12 tells us that hope deferred makes the heart sick. Defer means to put off until later. When hope is put off until later it makes our hearts sick. So if hope is understood as our wants for what we don't have yet, we develop a sick heart. This pushes us to strive and live chasing instead of living to receive.

Hope is here because we are in. We are in that flow of Father's goodness. We are in His love. We are in His present, current state of victory. We are on the "inside", not on the "outside". Life has a lot for us to do, but doing it from receiving is totally different than doing it chasing. Harmony. Peace. A settled place inside. These unlock much more productivity than dissonance, fear and anxiety.

Enjoy the good gifts coming toward you from Father. You're already in. You have hope. Let your heart be settled. You already have what is of highest importance. You have Christ in you and you in Christ. You are a new creation with the hope of glory; not the wanting of glory we don't have, but the fullness of glory resident through Christ.

> **So if hope is understood as our wants for what we don't have yet, we live with a sick heart.**

Take some time to process this understanding and let your mind renew to this reality. Live in harmony. Live FROM, not trying to GET TO. Watch your productivity, creativity, progress, dreaming, and advancing increase as you live IN rest (success). When we realize we are IN and already HAVE (possess), boldness is the natural result.

Receive boldly!

Your Notes ::

Before and After ::

Is your life spent chasing or receiving?

HOPE = BOLD

"Love hopes all things..."

1 Corinthians 13:7

Day 7 - *The Source*

To understand hope as a present reality rather than a want or a wish to obtain later, we have to look at hope's source. It doesn't seem like that would be much of an issue. Yet the general use of the word hope and how so many never really experience the force of hope points to the need to look a little deeper. Since hope is a reality, we have to ask where it comes from. Taking the time to consider and to let it reshape our thinking, opens the glories of that reality.

Apostle Paul says hope is what we have (2Corinthians 3:12). Usually hope is seen as something needed. That is because hope is usually seen as something of which we are the source. Often, many view hope as something we create inside our emotions or thoughts. It's easy to see how optimism and hope get confused. Optimism is positive feelings or a positive sense about something. Optimism has the opportunity to fluctuate depending on our emotional or mental state of being. Optimism is something we are able to produce. Some more easily than others.

> **You're not the source of hope. You're the recipient of hope.**

When hope is understood in the mindset of optimism, we make hope something we produce or muster up. Hope then becomes a fluctuating situation that is determined by our emotional or mental situation. This leaves us on unstable ground. Once again, this makes

You already have hope

us the source for our hope. So the days we can't manage to get up enough emotional strength, we buy into the deception we don't have hope or it's hopeless. The truth is that you have hope. You just might not have internal strength to be optimistic.

So when we embrace hope as the reality we have and understand it's the unconditional assurance Father's goodness prevails, you get to receive from a Source outside of your internal strength. When the present reality of hope becomes your awareness, it provides boldness to face situations or approach life in a secure way that fuels positive thinking and optimism. Hope becomes a force of strength giving you what's needed. That's much different than you needing to muster up hope. You are not the source of hope. You are the recipient of hope. Hope becomes your source, not you the source of hope.

See this differently and let it renew your awareness that Father's love is everlasting and from that love hope is sourced. Love releases hope (1 Corinthians

13:7). You are already loved so you already have hope (2 Corinthians 3:12). Rest in that reality so it gives you what you can't give yourself.

Love is the source of hope.
Hope is the source of boldness.

Your Notes ::

Before and After ::
How loved do you feel?

"And there was evening and there was morning..."

Genesis 1:5

Day 8 - *Start After Rest*

In Genesis we see God created night and then day. It tells us that His design is that we begin in rest and then start. To give us clarity, the concept of rest must not be understood as idleness or no action. Rest is a state of being, not an absence of activity. Rest is a place of settledness and internal ease. We can be very busy and productive and be at rest. Actually, I believe you will have fuller productivity and achievement living from rest. Most are chasing rest. They say they're "living for the weekend". But we can be in rest every day. We should start from rest. Rest is embracing the full joy of satisfaction. After creation, God rested (Genesis 2:2). He didn't become inactive or detached. He experienced His full joy in being satisfied that His goodness was displayed in a creation that was good and in mankind who is very good (Genesis 1:31).

So once creation was set, we're told there was rest. In our modern culture, that feels like rest came at the end. It actually was the start. It was the "night" leading to the "day". Whether someone holds strictly to a literal concept of 7 days of creation or is open to it being metaphoric, if we take the framework of our calendar week away, we can see God brought forth and set up things for man. Then once man was in place, rest was the 1st step for man. Just as in God making night and then day, man's first moment started on the "Day of Rest", and then moved into productivity. God and man were not separated. So when we are told on the 7th day God rested (Genesis 2:2), man was at rest as well.

When we embrace the present reality of hope, our hearts and minds become aware of His goodness in ways that answer deep questions that often give us internal insomnia (which is a strong reason for the struggle of physical insomnia). Without the unconditional assurance of Father's goodness we

Hope turns over false images of God

are in a constant demand to perform. We are restless. We have to embrace the reality of Father's goodness so our souls can receive the joy of satisfaction. From that, we bring forth all we have the potential for.

Without embracing the reality of hope, we are often like the prophets of Baal at Mt Carmel (1 Kings 18) who spent all day in exhausting performance mode flailing and beating around, our hearts live under the weight of having to be enough or do enough to get God to respond. Elijah in this account shows us rest. He was strongly engaged in making a difference, but he was at rest, assured he didn't have a performance requirement to get God's involvement. He had an unconditional assurance Father was already involved because He's good. That ended up overturning idols and false images of God. Hope turns over false images of God and sets us in the place of rest so we are most prepared to start.

When you live in hope, it puts you in rest. From that, we engage boldly. Not in a life of performance to get something from God, but releasing what we already know we have from God. There was night and then day. There was Day 7 and then Day 8. Rest leads to the best start.

Be bold enough to live in rest!

Your Notes ::

Before and After ::

Where do you need to adjust your view of God and understand He is for you not against?

"Trust..."

Proverbs 3:5

HOPE = BOLD

Day 9 - *Trust*

We access hope via trust. Dealing with hope requires us to evaluate trust. In our Day 3 study, I briefly shared the options we have in where to place our trust. Because trust is so vital and often so broken, let's consider more on this day's study.

When our mind is renewed to the present reality of hope, instead of it being our wishes for the future, we then have to ask if our trust is set on what is here and available now. Do we trust His goodness is toward us and present among us? This is often where the rubber meets the road. Our hearts want hope because we are built for hope. Our need for hope is in our soul's DNA. Besides our need to understand biblical hope more accurately, the other major challenge for us is to face trust issues. Whatever level of trust we assert, will be the level of hope we enjoy. Hope results from love. When we embrace love, trust then becomes our access to hope.

> **Trust is how we embrace hope.**

Trust is so challenging because it requires living in the unknown. Since love trusts, love is ok with the unknown because love hopes all things (1 Corinthians 13). Love creates the unconditional assurance Father's goodness prevails. Since hope is that assurance, we have a solid reality to put our trust. Trust is how we embrace hope. It's a revolving result of love. Because Jesus showed us Father is good and is happy with us, it becomes a knowing that makes us ok with the unknown. That is trust. Seeing hope creates trust and trust holds to hope.

Our natural fear of the unknown, added to the amount of times our trust is broken, becomes a strong mixture holding us from the vulnerable place of trust. So we more easily convey hope as a wish, but a wish is a want without passion. A wish doesn't demand much from us. A wish doesn't make us vulnerable. It doesn't require trust. With a wish we are able to keep things pushed off to some future time so we don't have to engage trust in what we currently have in Father's goodness. If all Jesus provided is "coming" instead of "here", we just live waiting instead of having.

Trust is how we move from waiting to having. Trust navigates us through the unknown by embracing hope as a present reality of an unconditional assurance Father's goodness prevails. Trust is ok with the unknown in front of us because it knows something secure: Father's goodness. Hope has always been and always will be, but our trust becomes the capacity in how much we hold to hope.

Our minds can adjust to a new understanding of hope and our hearts can embrace hope is here, but our trust must be engaged so we gain something more than knowledge.

Trust is how we move from waiting to having.

Where is your trust? What degree of trust are you living? What healing is needed for you to vulnerably trust so you receive the most out of hope? Take the needed time to talk with Father about trusting His goodness, by seeing Jesus and following Spirit. I don't want you reading this and coming to a new understanding without living the results hope provides. That happens through trust. Become increasingly unafraid of the unknown by a deep trust in the known - Father's goodness is fully toward you. His goodness isn't something yet to come. It's here.

Boldly trust!

Your Notes ::

Before and After ::

What are your trust issues?

"What was brought to an end..."

2 Corinthians 3:13

Day 10 - *Brought to an End*

To go forward in anything, there is often the need to let go of, or come to the end of a previous thing. It's been said in sport's circles that you can't get to second base until you leave first. To move forward in living bold through hope, there are some areas of thinking that will need to come to an end. These 10 days have been giving you truths to unlock you from mindsets that held you back. I want this 10ᵗʰ day of study to zero in on seeing certain mindsets ended.

Hope has always been there.

Apostle Paul in 2 Corinthians 3:13 states, "the outcome of what was being brought to an end". One verse prior, he states, "we have this hope". You will have to spend time examining and considering what mindsets or preconceived thoughts you have about God and yourself that will need to end so you can step fully into the hope available to you.

Hope has always been there. Hope is a reality you can live in. Hope is not something you need to get. Hope is what you need to increasingly become aware of. Hope is here! An unconditional assurance Father's goodness prevails is available to you. Living hope will most likely require some mindsets coming to an end.

Let me offer some mindsets that you might hold that need to end:

- God holding judgement over you so you will obey
- God needing to be appeased so He is no longer angry with you
- Hope is your ability to think positively
- Believing you have to get more hope
- The idea your hope goes up or down

Perhaps that most significant mindset that needs to end is: Deferred Hope.

Hope isn't to be put off until later. That becomes the source of sick hearts (Proverbs 13:12). Hope is what you currently have. Hope is what you have forever!

Bringing mindsets to an end comes by beholding the true Jesus without the veil created by the Law (2 Corinthians 3:14). Being in Spirit instead of the law is the key to living without a veil, or distortion which traps hearts. 2 Corinthians 3:14 explains how the law veils hearts even after Jesus did all He did.

Paul's statements in 2 Corinthians 3 are aimed at ending the "veils" keeping us from embracing we have hope. Being Spirit-lead not law-lead is how we live in the freedom found in the greater glory of Father's goodness instead of the dimming glory of the condemning Law (2 Corinthians 3).

> **We see His goodness covers us and seals us in order to seat us.**

You and I must be those who see the control of the Law's performance-based demands come to an end and live the full life of hope brought in Spirit. Father has always wanted sons and daughters living by His voice, not slaves living a list of lifeless requirements. He wants us around His table hearing and knowing Him, not out in the fields slaving and wondering if we've done enough (Luke 15).

Slaving in fields and wallowing in pig pens needs to end (Luke 15). There is an open seat at the table, and it is yours. Thinking He doesn't want you there or you can't be there until you get cleaned up or get enough done, must come to an end. In Jesus' parable of the Running Father (Luke 15), we're told Father did what was needed, not the Prodigal Son. This is the reality of hope. This is how we see hope differently. We see His goodness covers us and seals us, in order to seat us. A robe, a ring, a chair are His love given to us. It's not something we are waiting on. It's what we have.

Hope is here! Be bold!

Your Notes ::

Before and After ::

How much do you live with hope deferred?

"But be transformed by the renewal of your mind,"

Romans 12:2

Conclusion:

To experience newness in anything, we must come to new understanding and then new practice. When we think differently, we can live free. These 10 days have given you valuable ground work to live boldly because you have hope. As you read over and over, your thinking will be renewed and become even more aware of Father's goodness. Seeing Father's goodness and love that is already toward you is the key. Ending old ways of understanding and pursuing deeper measures of realizing how Jesus displayed Father will bring forth such a difference.

My aim has been to give you Father, unveil hope, and provoke you to embrace more of what you already have. I pray you ongoingly gain from this book and invite others into a new reality.

Access all we have available for those in The Hope Revolution at:

www.wearethehopeful.com

#HOPEequalsBOLD #theHOPErevolution
#HopeIsHere #wearethehopeful

35198996R00061

Made in the USA
Columbia, SC
20 November 2018